Snapshots of Life

Margaret Karim

By Margaret karim

ISBN
Hardbound-978-621-470-882-6

MOBI/KINDLE-978-621-470-883-3

Softbound/Paperback-978-621-470-884-0

Published by:

Poetry Planet Book Publishing House

Rosario, Pozorrubio, Pangasinan, Philippines

Contact Number: 09554960094

DEDICATION

In loving memory of my parents, Tom pet and Elodia Smith and, my brother Anthony.

FOREWORD

I began writing poetry and sharing to Facebook groups in August 2020. It was a pastime. Did not have any expectations.

Found myself on a whirlwind creative journey, culminating in this book. Thank you Poetry Planet for encouraging me to believe in myself. Forever grateful.

TABLE OF CONTENTS

CHARACTER POEMS

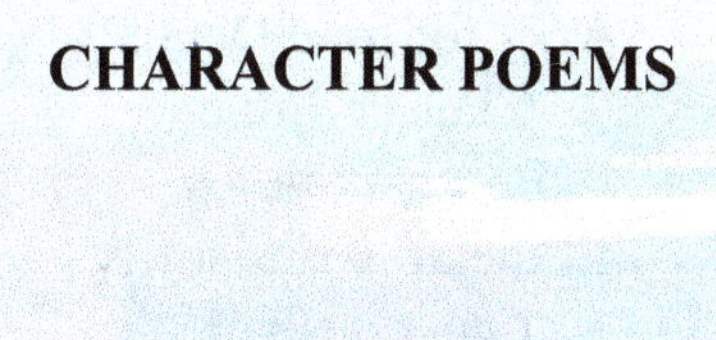

SILENCE

Dowager Hotel
Elements of mystique
Decaying grandeur
Shabby chic
Woman in black
Arrives at midnight
Claret lips
Dress skin tight
Sits by piano
Asks for tune Debus
Clair de Lune
Poignant notes
Fill the air Cries softly
Quiet despair
Bar empties Left alone
Moonlight gleams
On silent phone

NOSTALGIA

Beehive hair
Raspy throat
Black eyeliner
Musty fur coat
Port and lemon
Preferred tipple
Always orders
Generous triple
Fake Rolex on wrist
Belonged to her
Ken lived the good life
Way back when
Sighs at life today
Breakdown of Society
Broken marriages
Two to a penny
Sips her drink
Dwells on past
Long may it last?

LIVES HER WAY

Vintage biker's jacket
Boots thigh high
Tartan pashmina
Sartorial rules don't apply
Black eyeliner just so
Long gray hair
Artfully arranged topknot
Sophisticated air
Antique pearls
One amber hoop earring
Silver bangles
Forever tinkling
Drinks champagne
Occasionally swears
Talks with her hands
Mediterranean flair
Raucous laugh
Energizes everyone
Ageing disgracefully
Determined on fun
Edging nine decades
Lives her way
Done so all her life
Proud to say

DISAPPEARING ACT

He is a quiet man
Sits at the bar alone
Designer suit
Subtle cologne
Polite to all
Exchanges chit chat
No use expecting
More than that
Subtle way
Of deflecting curiosity
Dismissing a person
Simultaneously
Lack of warmth
In opaque green eyes
Hints at danger
In fragile disguise
Self-contained air
Women find appealing
Brushes them aside
Uninterested in flirting
Is at work you see
Waiting patiently
Month undercover
Finally ready
Sips his whisky
Good selection here
Pity that after act
He must disappear

IRISH COFFEE

She is cream
Swirled into Irish coffee
Cool, sensuous
Aesthetically pleasing
Air of self-containment
Prohibits my approach
I watch from a distance
Unwilling to encroach
Dresses in vintage clothing
Art Deco attire
Swirling, flowing lines
I cannot help but admire
Enters café at midday
Orders tea and toast
Always same meal
My staple roast
Sit in respective corners
Lost in individual thought
Occasionally our eyes meet
Her's, striking peridot
Today she wanders over
My heart misses a beat
Carries her plate, cup
Takes opposite seat

SILENT GOODBYE

Woman in black
Sips a cappuccino
Gentle eyes
Ingrained sorrow
Accepted her role
In his life
Never asked for more
Or gave him strife
Understanding nature?
Perhaps a fool?
Does not matter
Agreed to his rules
Neither foresaw
Present scenario
Unexpected death
Heard via the radio
Important man illicit affair
Grieves alone
Private loss to bear
Public farewell
Knows only one way
Pays for her coffee
Stands outside the café
Funeral cortege
Passes by
Respectfully bows
Mouths a silent goodbye

DIVA

My name is Lola Dove
I sang opera
It was my life
I was a Diva
You won't remember
My rise to fame
Resulting publicity
Wondrous acclaim
I was young once
Beautiful like you
Charming, capable
Believe me, true
You perceive
A shriveled husk
Lost in faded memories
Often brusque
I feel so vulnerable
Now I am old
Dependent on others
Doing what I am told
By chits like you
Don't want charity
Concealed disdain
Or your pity
I am not "dear,
Lol, Loli, or love"
Impudent girl
My name is Lola Dove

THE FRENCH PIANIST

The pianist is a fixture
Been at Joey's years
Ask him for any tune
Plays it by ear
Faded elegance
0lde world charm
Gentle smile
Professional calm
Softly spoken
Small talk his forte
Curiosity follows him
Politely bats it away
Women show interest
Make clear intent
Graciously declines offers
In his French accent
Works late shift
Six evenings a week
Sundays at home
Lonely, bleak
Sits in bedsit
After visiting cemetery
Lost in reminiscences
Toasts his wife's memory

IRREVOCABLE

Alone in her bedroom
Crying, forlorn
Smudged make up
Wedding dress unworn
Believed in promises
Like a naive adolescent
Invested dreams
In that garment
On a hanger
Caught by breeze
Gently swirls
As if to tease
Buries her face
Silky folds
Heart caught
Stranglehold
Hears parents
Murmured conversation
Attempts to make sense
Of situation
Footsteps stop
At her close door
Mother knocked
She ignores
Phone rings again
Never who she hopes
Fingers crossed
Emotions on tightrope
Continued belief
In his return absurd
Goodbye irrevocable
Meant every word

FAVOURITE FRAGRANCE

She roared into my life
Confidence on display
Attitude in her stride
Enticing sashay
Wore red stilettos
Matching lipstick too
Encircling one wrist
Rose bracelet tattoo
Sat at my side
Local bistro
My mouth feel open
Cartoonish O Smiled at me
Mimed closing my jaw
Said she did not bite
Or have grasping claws
Told me to breathe
Scent of adventure
Still my favourite fragrance
Three decades later

ANONYMITY

He sits in a corner
Liveiy beach bar
At his feet Battered guitar
Whisky on table
Roll up in hand
On left wrist
Faded leather band
Kind smile for all
Exudes cairn
Distinctive voice
Soothing balm Soft, deep drawl
Undertones of honey
Enter its sphere
Yearn to hear his story
Ask a personal question
Changes subject politely
Departs at end of evening
Cloaked in anonymity

SURVIVOR

Sits at usual table
In comforting shadow
Lit by soft candlelight
Framed by a window
Smudged lipstick
Ruby stained cigarette
Black backless dress
Tumbler of anisette
Life often cruel
Suffered consequences
Traces left behind
Visible vestiges
But she is not a victim
Eyes spark fire
Glints of strength,
Humour, passion, desire

OI' CEE

Seagulls swoop
Over a tranquil sea
Surrounding marina
Whirl of activity
Gossip abounds
Excitement in air
There she is!
Blue streaked hair
Cigarette holder in hand
Trailing puffs of smoke
Dramatic As ever
Attired a la baroque
Missed by all
Lively spirit contagious
Away too long
Flamboyant, outrageous
OI' Cee is back
Intent on fun
Chandelier earrings
Glitter in sun
Glides to favorite bar
Orders neat whisky
Asked where she has been
Winks mischievously

IMPRINT

Scotty's Bar
Night I will never forget
She called me over
To light her cigarette
My fingers trembled
She held them steady
Looked me in eyes
Unexpected affinity
Warmth, affection
Familiar stranger
Old souls reunited?
Destined adventure?
Small town mind
Encountered sophistication
Windows of possibility opened
Views to new expectations
She woke me at sunrise
Gentle kiss on forehead
Imprinted sweet memory
And left my bed

RARE

Atop vestiges
Of past grief
Amber eyes
Hint at mischief
Gentle expression
Beguiles sensual lips
Readily smile
Partial to icy voignior
And emotive violin
Listening to latter
Goosebumps skin
Innate observation list
Sensitive to nuances
Generosity of spirit
Truly amazes
She is woman
At heart a child Strong, innocent
A tad wild
Admitted into embrace
Treat with care
Appreciate worth
She is rare

COMPASSION

Tender prey
Child of Universe
Dressed in rags
Handed coins
From designer bags
People pass
Rarely meet her eyes
Not difficult
To understand why
Unsavory problems In Society
Should not form part
Of daily reality
Best watched on social media
Or wide-screen TV
Discussed in a warm pub
Over supper, with family
Meanwhile, she sits Tender prey
For any predator
Who happens her way?
Street life terrifying
Feels so alone
Yet, preferable, safer
To returning home

WRONG ROAD

No, not asking
For a dime
Beg a moment,
Of your time
Please see me
As I was before
Still am
At my core
Don't allow
My addiction
To provoke
An adverse reaction,
Or distract from
My beating heart
I am not
A filthy upstart,
Just a person with
Burdens to unload,
Who took
The wrong road
Lost my way
None of us immune,
If Fate considers Path opportune
Thank you for listening
Even with half an ear
I know you long
To disappear
Uncomfortable
To face reality
Become aware
Dregs of society

Might have been you
Instead of me
No, keep your coins,
Grant me dignity

LOVING VIGIL

Shabby coat
Spotlessly clean
Worn black shoes
Polished to a gleam
Rising wind
Dark clouds gather
Thunder, lightning
Drenching rain shower
Abandoned railway station
Pervading stench
Perches cross legged
Rotting wooden bench
Increasingly bedraggled
Does not complain
Waits patiently
For his train
Lives in a parallel world
Fragile reality
Destroying illusion
Inconceivable to family
Daughter or son
Always at a distance
Loving vigil
Daily occurrence

A WORLD APART

Pink tinged sky
Burnt orange glow
Fast pace of day
Gradually slows
Welcoming restaurants
Fringe village square
Candlelit tables
In open balmy air
Hum of conversation
Interspersed with laughter
Rises, tinkles
Into ether
Fragrance of jasmine
Surrounds
Diners enveloped
Invisible cloud
Crescent moon appears
Twinkling stars inviting ambience
Perceived from afar
As dispossessed
Hidden in plain sight
Huddle down
For the night

MY SHOES

Slip on my skin
Before you criticize
Blink, then see,
With my eyes Perceive,
Understand reasons,
Logic behind
My actions
Now, take my shoes,
Wear them one day
Walk in my steps Just a little way

LEGACY

My mother passed on
A verbal legacy
Handed down
By her late Daddy
These wise words;
My child aim high
Chase dreams
Allow imagination to fly
But, on life's journey,
Pause occasionally
Savor blessings
Reflect on humility
Never lose sight
Of your humanity
Offer less fortunate
Compassion, empathy

HAIKUS

Beauty unsurpassed
Divineiy crafted Nature
Ever may it last?

Goiden grains of sand
Trickie through toes and tickie
Soft summer kisses

Undulating clouds
Billowy cotton pillows
A tender caress

Majestic oak tree
Surrounded by autumn leaves
Glowing gold carpet

Glorious silence
Melody like no other
The clear notes of peace

Poignant sound
Spade clangs
Prepares ground
Sky darkens
Violent squall
Clouds burst
Rain falls
Downpour Staccato beat
Accompanies coffin
Final retreat
One more lost

To eternal sleep
Bagpipes play
Mourners weep

INHUMANITY

Futile
Centre of town
Gated community
Hallowed ground
Naval cemetery
Ancient headstones
Crumbling words
Young lives forsaken
Humanity absurd
Never learns from past
Discards lessons
Enduring lust for power
Repeated abominations
Difficult to accept
Futile pondering why
Century after century
Innocents continue to die
One more
In the distance

CONFLICT

Homes rubble
Lives torn apart
Photos of dead children
Clutched to mothers hearts
Power, greed, corruption
Poison air
Injustice rules
Suffering everywhere
Nothing changes
Generation after generation
Human beings disposable
Global ethos of civilization
Humility, empathy
Left to the few
Patch up destruction
Until next conflict brews

WE WEEP

He surveys the world
Eyes veiled by age
Replays of inhumanity
Centre stage
Sees children's hopes fade
Wither, die
Destroyed at incipience
Without knowing why
Logical explanation?
Never has been
Egos, since time began,
Their spin
Narcissistic minds
Twisting reality
Benefitting the few
To hell with the majority
Powerless, we join him,
Weep at continuing insanity

BLIND

Remains a child
Trusting, guileless
Views the world
Haze of tenderness
Gentle, kind
Spirit bare
Unwilling to believe
Predators out there
Pursuing self-interest
Acting myriad parts
Exploiting goodness
Draining pure hearts
Excuses bad behavior
Espouses explanations
Miserable childhoods
Traumatic provocations
Unable to accept truth
Blind to stark reality
Some people care little
For honesty, decency

LOST GENERATION

Souls stand to attention
Dutiful unto eternity
Salute at ghostly planes
As they fly with fluidity
Suspended in limbo
An entire generation
Existing in a field
Of denied expectations
Fluttering innocence
Destroyed at initiation
By the rallying cry
Of warring Nations
Forgotten voices
Blow in the wind
Vestiges of a fate
Predetermined
Premature death in a row
Humanity screams
Incomprehensible vista
Graveyard of lost dreams

SHE IS NOT THERE

Escapes parents
Disintegrating lives
Confusing world Bitterness, lies
Does not understand
New reality
Wishes they explained
Requires certainty
Neither see her
She is not there
Could it be
They no longer care?
Heads for oak tree
Its majestic canopy
Curls on undergrowth
Listens to Nature's symphony
Bird song, rustle of Leaves
Predictable continuity
Aching heart attains
Temporary security

JOIN ME

Beloved Gaia,
I see your despair
Anguish at realizing
Few care
Bewildered eyes watch
Habitats violated
Sacred creation
Taken for granted
Foresee further greed
Cloaked in progress
Fauna, flora sacrificed
More children in distress
I bend in prayer
Under my verdant canopy
As each of my siblings
Expires prematurely
Join me, my mother Murmur
Hope's lullaby
For it is not my time
I do not wish to die
Loss

LOSS

Inconceivable
Sepia photographs
Rocking chair
Patchwork throw
Surreal still air
I wander rooms
Absence tangible
Permanent reality
Inconceivable
Folded spectacles
Book half read
Both await you
On unmade bed

UNAWARE

She sits in a corner
Of her local café
Prefers to observe
Never has much to say
Orders aperitif
Before evening meal
Has little effect
Does not eat a great deal
Hungers for past
This, unavailable
Memories do not satisfy
Appetite insatiable
Watches others
With a benevolent eye
Living their lives
Unaware of time passing by
No thought of cruel
Fate Loneliness of an empty bed
As it should be
Planning ahead

MAKES DO

He reaches
To stroke her hair
Bed empty
She is not there
He hears
Witty banter
Calls out to share it
She does not answer
He opens fridge
Nothing appeals
Misses insistence
On home cooked meals
Part of him gone
Wanders aimlessly
He cries
Feels lonely
Craves her presence
Unique laugh
Makes do with useless
Memories, photographs

MEMORY LINGERS

Ashes scattered
Beneath oak tree
Peaceful spot
View of sea Armful of lilies
Held to his chest
Lays them down
Mama's place of rest
Beloved presence
In still air
Sudden breeze
Stirs his hair
Her memory
Oh, it lingers
Soothing touch
Gentle fingers

WHISPER OF YESTERDAY

Side of bed empty
Pile of books left unread
Future hopes unshared
Small talk's words unsaid
Misses his ungainly form
Making each room untidy
Every unique nuance
Of his complex personality
The ups and downs
Innate to shared life
Daily responsibilities
Role as a wife
All that remains is
A whisper of yesterday
Her heart grieves
Poignant memory

UNWELCOME REALITY

She sits alone
In a stained blouse
Surrounded by memories
Old family house
Walks around empty rooms
A few times a day
Listening to echoes
Of yesterday
Eldest son's laughter
Daughter singing
Younger boys squabbling
Husband mumbling Scents of past
Invade nose
Home cooking
Line blown clothes
Misses her old man
Faults and all
Puts on cheerful voice
When children call
No time for chit chat
Remind her they are busy
Brusque conversations
Discharging duty
Tells herself she understands
Does not in actuality
Increasing loneliness
Unwelcome reality

WHEN WE FIRST BEGAN

Dawn's filmy light
Your face on the pillow Illness blurred
Youthful profile in repose
Tell me you remember
When we were young
Promises of forever
Woven easily by tongues
Laughed at the idea
We would cease to be
No thought of tomorrow
Cruel mortality
Taut skin, strong heartbeats
Love brand new
Built a secure world
Inhabited by two
Foundations crumbling
Cannot even cry
Ability lost to me
As we say goodbye
Eager to revisit the past
Our special land
You smile in remembrance
Squeeze my hand
I move to lie next to you
And, together, on the divan,
Return for the last time,
To when we first began

IRRETRIEVABLY

Mind lost its moorings
Twilight world at sea
Vaguely aware thoughts
Steadily losing clarity
Time has little meaning
Blur of days, nights
Bewilderment to left
Confusion to right
Frustration rises
Anger follows behind
Yearn to express feelings
Words I cannot find
Familiar faces surround
Names a fading memory
Flickers of recollection
Tease occasionally
Instants of lucidity
Reveal sorrow in loving eyes
As the person I used to be
Slowly, irretrievably dies

YESTERDAY

Hand in hand
Little sister and I
Dressed in Sunday best
Bewildered eyes
Papa went for milk
Returned in a casket
Granny says he passed
Gives us each a biscuit
Preacher states Daddy
Now lives in sky
Yet Aunt
May announces
He's awaiting our goodbye
That man sure ain't
Papa lying there so still
Pasty, serious face
Cotton up one nostril
Nope, a mistake,
We are both agreed
Try to tell Mama
She pays us no heed
Adults say shush Shoo us away
We run into the yard
Weep for yesterday

MISCELLANEOUS

Ghostly remains
Halfway up winding hill
Monastery ruins decay
Surrounded by majestic oaks
Leaves whisper, branches sway
Muted sound of childish glee
Lingers in the cold damp air
Shadowy small forms move
Hide and seek without care
Haunting, poignant sadness
Pervades over all
Soft, as tender kisses,
Hazy rain begins to fall

RHAPSODY

Strains of nostalgia
Apparent within
Melody played
On battered violin
Forgotten memories
Escape on the breeze
Heir familiar notes
Intent on release
It's vibrant Composition
Awakens senses
Stirs emotions
Colorful, Tender rhapsody
Celebration of Personal history

VESTIGES

Velvet brilliance
Now shabbily attired
Creased, musty
No longer desired
Short lived heyday
Relegated to past
Faded memory
Gathering dust
Yet, innate elegance,
Continues to linger
In bent and withered
Arthritic fingers
Vestiges of grandeur
Crackle whispers
Release scented secrets
0f former adventures

REPRISE

Swirled whisky
Winks hello
Amber fireflies
Translucent glow Betrayal's taste
Residue lingers Sit quietly
Stir grate s embers
Cracking logs
Warming flames Alcohol drips
Grateful veins
Burred red lips
Sightless eyes
Bad memories
Set on reprise

GATHERING DUST

Mind's attic
Personal curios
Life experiences
Black and white photos
Conversation, laughter
Plain gold band
Youthful expectations
Bare left hand
Faded bouquet
Vestiges of distrust
Boxed memories
Gathering dust

MEDIEVAL TALE

Horses approach
Thunderous beat
Informer leaves inn
Inconspicuously retreats
Outside, cobbles glisten
Ethereal misty rain
He swiftly disappears
End of maleficent campaign
Children stop playing
Mothers' orders
Held to maternal bosoms
Huddle in corners
Sheriff, his men,
Stop at Meggie's door
Locals bow heads
At shouts of whore
Healer emerges
Familiar, gentle face
Herbalist known to all
County her birthplace
Officials push, shove
Intent on humiliation
Witch to be removed
Threat to population
Wrists, ankles shackled
Bound to Sheriff's steed
Neighbors impotent
Perilous to intercede

Procession leaves
Silent, tangible sorrow
Storm clouds explode
Grief's crescendo

NEIGHBORHOOD TALES

Family
A dutiful daughter
Does not question
Beliefs established
Over generations
Family is everything
Mantra since birth
Parental respect
Determines self-worth
My role by decree
Our Harbor café
Serving customers
As time slips away
I smile, chat
Avoid introspection
Discard dreams
At inception
Across the water
City lights glow
Promise a future
I will never know

DUSK'S SHADOW

Old neighborhood
Nostalgia in air
Dormant memories
Awaken, stir
Early childhood
Innocence, laughter
Dawn's promise
Of adventure
Sense of family
Blood link unnecessary
All folk united
In fortune, adversity
Jim's Café
Centre of activity
Indispensable
Hub of community
Times long gone
Life proceeds
Sows changes
Unfamiliar seeds
"Jimmy's" mourns
In dusk's shadows
Caved in roof
Boarded windows

DAWN ARRIVES

Late evening
Dim streetlight
Bar in alley
Hidden from sight
Candles at tables
Foggy window panes
Scent of inhaled herbs
Relaxation reigns
Soulful singer
Accompanied by piano
Alcohol flows
Flirtation in shadows
Town's forsaken and
Its beautiful people
Strangers during day
Nightly intermingle
Decadent ambience
Alternate conviviality
Dawn arrives
Return to reality

FOND FAREWELL

Breath slows
Mellow, deep
Old Zakaria
Drifts into sleep
Smiles wistfully
Hums the blues
Shabby bow tie
Worn tap shoes
Murmurs, dances
Internal beat
Yesterday's rhythm
Familiar, bittersweet
Music, steps
Unique duet
Tender memories
No regrets
Time to leave
Death's knell
Elderly feet glide
Bid fond farewell

RHYTHMS OF PAST

Duaint Town
Cobbled streets
Washing dries
In sultry heat
Lines of clothes
Dance in breeze
Outdoor performance
Smalls cavort, tease
Customs, traditions
Remain applicable
Modern society
In hospitable
Enthusiasm,
Excess In primary position
No time for minimalism
Sterile conditions
Change unwelcome
Long may it last
Native hearts beat
Rhythms of past

SNIPPETS OF CITY IIFE

Dawn breaks
A baby cries
Mother sings
A lullaby
Street sweeper
And his broom
Earphones on
Adjusts volume
Joggers, singly
And, in pairs,
Drink water
Gulp air
Young girl
Sated desire
Leaves a house
In evening attire
Elderly man
Behind glass
Recalls days
Street had class
In the distance
Church bells ring
Calling faithful
To decant sins

APPARITION

Misty rain
Smeared windows
Outdoors blurred
Light, shadows
Christmas Eve
Church bells ring
In the distance
Carolers sing
Sudden shiver
Goose pimpled skin

Grief surges
Tidal wave within
Under a lamp-post
Sees his silhouette
He blows a kiss
Performs a pirouette
Figure disperses
Was he there?
Feels a gentle flutter
His lips on her hair

ABSOLUTION

Lights a cigarette
Watches it glow
Wonders if
She will show
Never knows

If she will appear
But, each night,
Finds him here
Where she died
Long ago
Moment of madness
Alcohol fuelled ego
No excuses
Committed crime
Served His time
Has he paid
Retribution?
Seeks total
Absolution Ears prick
Cobble stones echo
Familiar sound
Of her stilettos

FINAL RIDE

Abandoned railway
Childhood home at rear
Engine approaches
Train almost here
Nostalgia
Lingers in air
Family reminiscences
Painful to bear
Eggs for breakfast
Sunny side up
Papa drinking tea
From favorite cup
Helping sell tickets
Sweeping fallen leaves
Mama preparing sandwiches
Tomato, ham, cheese
Velocity of overnight freights
Perceived mystique
Promise of excitement
Penetrating deep sleep
Innocent times
Mum, Dad, long departed
Unknown destination
Soul broken hearted
Now his turn to board
Final ride
Finds his parents
Waiting inside

DISSATISFACTION

Veil of misty rain
All around
Slippery cobbles
On the ground
Old Town enveloped
In hazy light
Atmospheric winter's night
Wears a red raincoat
Enviable style
Full figured sashay
Visible from a mile
Aware of hostile stares
From passersby
Naked envy in
Some prying eyes
Accustomed to gossip
Its constant presence
Has developed
An air of insouciance
Learned to brush
Negative interest aside
Understands self-assurance
Leaves others dissatisfied

PERSONAL

I am
I am my Mother's child
Her essence lives in me
Strength, compassion
An enduring legacy
Her blood courses
Through my veins
Nurture, protect all,
Echoing refrain
Eternal love resides
In her memory
Accompanies, comforts
In adversity
Her generosity,
Empathy inviolate,
Innate tenderness,
Kindling for my spirit
Her earthly remains,
Under an oak tree piled
Our souls forever aligned
I am my Mother's child

MUM

Time moves on
Not for me
Same place
Life empty
Decade later
Increasingly alone
Cannot accept
You are gone
Go through motions
Every day
Do so for others
Pretend I am okay
Yearn to float
Above the sky
See beyond
Sight of eye
Feel your energy
Tender embrace
Confirm you exist
In another space

DAD

One off eccentric
Beloved to friends, family
Five years after passing
They smile at your memory
Intelligent, sensitive,
Non-judgmental, kind
Benefit of doubt
Uppermost in mind
Funny, unassuming,
Deceptively shy
In the right company
Waved inhibition goodbye
Enjoyed singing,
Never low key,
In church, crowded lifts,
If tipsy, at karaoke
Opera, writing, football
Abiding passions in later years
Embraced fashion
Conservative attire
Given the sack
Replaced by blousons,
And sorbet colored slacks
Dad, miss your presence,
Goodness, generosity,
Lack of tolerance
For injustice and envy,
Our irreverent conversations,
Shared sentimentality
You left knowing
All you meant to me if

Heaven exists
There you will be
Resting in peace
With Mum and Anthony

FOR ANTHONY

When we were young
I kept you from harm
Fought for your rights
Ensured you were warm
You took on mantle
Protected me from unkind
Made them accountable
You, younger brother
The light of our lives
Travelled with darkness
Hidden deep inside
And when you died
Too young; not even fifty
It destroyed the dynamic
Of our close, loving family
Leaving us
Unable to breath
Too damaged
Too grieve
Sorrow infiltrated
Our everyday
And our parents
Began a slow decay

BY STEALTH

Death took them too
And now
They reside with you
At times, I close my eyes
Will my soul to let go
Fly to your embrace
As I miss you all so

SNAPSHOTS OF MY IIFE

Roses, emeralds
Cheesecake, champagne
Sunlit white villages
Of southern Spain
A stranger's smile
Loved one's embrace
Dog's unwieldy tongue
Washing my face
Glorious sunsets
Gospel chorus
Children shrieking
Just because
Teenagers breathing
Hormonal, hedonistic air
Seniors nostalgic view
On past errors
Rock of Gibraltar
Unconditional love
Ancestral whispers
Heard from above
Effervescent laughter
Grief's lonely tears
Snapshots of my life
Collected over years

A KINDER EARTH

My child
Best of me
In her blood
Courses history
Dreams
Of past generations
Entwined
With future aspirations
Combined hopes
A thread of unity
Interwoven in each
Maternal tapestry
Our children
Given love, worth
Will work towards
A kinder earth

REGRETS

Where are you now
Burnt orange sunset
Carved into memory
Close my eyes
Revisit its beauty
Our moment
Of happenstance
Under striated sky
Wrapped in romance
Fleetingly
Our spirits aligned
Meaning of life
Redefined
Your tender essence
Resides in mind
Where are you now
Has life been kind?

WISH

She woke me
To watch sunrise
I turned away
Closed my eyes
She asked me
To walk in the rain
I shook my head
Called her insane
She told me
I feel alone
Did not listen
Now she has gone
My life empty
Heart harbors regret
Wish her at my side
To see sunset

INNUMERABLE

Spicy cologne
Old tweed jacket
Gentle fingers
Fastening my bracelet
Heartfelt laughter
Bony ankles
Polite manners
Summer freckles
Tender touch
Curious expression
Tuneless voice
Interesting conversations
Loving, affectionate
Perfect confidant
Inconceivable
We should ever part
Ultimately incompatible
You could not stay
But, oh, I miss you,
Innumerable ways

MISTAKE

On stormy days
Walks by shore
Seagulls circle
Angry waves roar
Wild wind blows
Ruffles his hair
Seawater spray
Refreshes air
Droplets mingle with tears
Still misses her
After all these years
Radiant smile
Tender caress Sense of humor
Her presence
Made a mistake
Left her behind
But she is never
Far from mind

CONSCIENCE

You left
Do not blame you
Wish I had
That choice too
To chase dreams
Follow desires
Light myriad
Hedonistic fires
Explore
Drift, fly
Me, me, me
In mind's eye
But, my conscience,
Understands reality
Tethers me
To responsibility
Accept role
Embrace it Happy Your spirit
Has freedom to ascend
Touch infinity Reach beyond
Yet, occasionally I reflect
On my circumstances
And my soul yearns
To exchange places

RELATIONSHIPS

Alibi
I glimpsed a scene
Of your family life
You kissed your children
Smiled at your wife
Instigated a group hug
Held on tight
Tickled your son
He wriggled in delight
Unhappy at home!
Why did you lie?
Next time you cheat
Find another alibi

MODERN CINDERELLA

Drop off kids
Go to work
Minimum wage
Smile at jerks
Collect children
Sole control
Autopilot the evening
Exhaustion on hold
Ring your parents
Ensure they are fine
Mum is lonely
Keeps you on line
Call over
Mind preoccupied
Endless obligations
Push guilt aside
Prepare for tomorrow
All now in place
Commencement
Of daily rat race
Modern Cinderella
Sweep the floor Go to bed
Dream of more

IF ONLY

I catch you weeping
Ask if you are okay
You smile, nod, turn
Walk away
Eyes bleak
Pretend all is fine
Go to the fridge
Pour glass of wine
Sit at table
Enveloped in sadness
Tangible
I feel powerless
We once talked fluently
Trustworthy companions
Discussed nothing, all,
At ease sharing emotions
Now two strangers
Parody of pantomime
Lack of communication
Corroding your spirit, mine
If only you could allow
Entry into your mind
Not push me aside
Offers of help declined

GUILTY PLEASURE

We sit in my car
Sip warm white wine
Homage to old days
When he was mine
Play Dusty Springfield
On repeat
Savor memories
Souls complete

Forget his spouse
Temporarily Bury guilt
Momentarily
Talk of hindsight,
Regrets, cruel Fate,
Daily concerns,
Our illicit dates
Caress with wonder
Yearn for yesterday
A return to the past
Forewarned by today
Time to stop music
Head back to reality
He opens the door
Once again, leaves me

AS LOVE'S EMBERS DIE

I see your silhouette
By open window
Muslin curtains
Dance around you
Sensing my presence
You turn towards me
Trembling with emotion
Hugging yourself tightly
Seeking negation of truth
Denial of reality
I shake my head
Heart weeping sadly
Outside the ocean
Murmurs its lullaby
Attempts to soothe
As love's embers die

PLEDGE

Will you trust me
Take a chance
Step into my arms
Lifetime's dance
Let us be realistic
Fate bound to surprise
Test convictions
Send Devils in disguise

All I can promise
Should passion diminish?
Is stir its vestiges
Seek to establish
Enduring companionship
Value its roots
Watch love evolve
Allow it to permute
And if our relationship
Cannot be repaired
Pledge to treasure memory
Of first twirl we shared

WON'T BE SWAYED

You touch me
Stir buried emotion
I am scared
Of rising passion
It tickles, bubbles
Under my skin

I hold myself tightly
Keep it within
Do not wish to feel
Once more care
Live life with hope
Lay myself bare
Past wounds crusted
With dead dreams
Further disappointment
Will newly burst seams
Your fingers are gentle
Attempt to persuade
I push them aside
Won't be swayed

IF I

If I stumble
Will you break my fall?
Or carry on walking
Not notice at all
If I touch you
Will you respond gently?
Or push me aside
Quickly and firmly
If I cry
Will you wipe my tears?
Or leave me alone
With unspecified fears
If I say his name
Will you react normally?
Or stop what you're doing
Tense visibly
If I accuse you
Will you answer truthfully?
Or lie
Turn your back abruptly

SHADES OF LOVE

Love is
You mimic accents
Make me laugh
I indulge your passion
For old photographs
You run my bath
Add bubbling potions
I listen to your
Crazy notions
We occasionally converse
Usually chit chat
Mutually dislike
Next doors brat
You kiss my forehead in bed each night
I reply sweet dreams
Turn off the light
We spoon
Comfortable together
Or, embrace passion,
One for the other
Sometimes we argue
Over trivialities
Soon apologies
Return to our normality
Compromise, respect
Loving companions
United, we two,
By enduring affection

LOVE'S LANGUAGE

You are fond
Of my flaws
Kiss me
Just because
Hold me
If I cry
Truly want
To know why
Insist on dancing
In evening rain
Accompanied by
Icy champagne
Which we down
In delight
Naming planets
Under moonlight
You say destiny
Brought is together
Urge me to believe
In forever
And I do, as you,
Gave me courage
To once more speak
Love's language

ROLE REVERSAL

They sit by the sea
Hand in hand
Lost in reminiscences
Both understand
Gaze unseeingly
At wondrous view
As former memories
Mingle with new
His youthful self
Selfish, impatient
Deriving pleasure
Calling her ancient
Her defense
Of bad behavior
Childish delight
In shared humor
She taught independence
Set him free
Backseat presence
His security
Elderly now
Losing her balance
Requires full time
Assistance
Tires of telling her
She is not an obligation
Her strength of character
Source of admiration
She stands holds his arm
Afraid to fall
Now he is the parent
Does not matter at all

TOMORROW

From our bedroom window
I watch you dance alone
Lost to a rhythm
Composed by your soul
I want to join you
Twirl into infinity
Those days over
You are a stranger to me
Tomorrow you cast
Our past aside
I will become a memory
No longer by your side
Your quest is adventure
To find yourself too
Did not realize there was
A missing part to you
If you ultimately discover
I am your destiny
Return to my arms
Here I will be

CAPTURED

Sun warmed sea
Glowing cerulean sky
Puffs of undulating clouds
Sensuously drift by
We float, minds at peace,
Hearts beat an adagio
Bodies caressed
Water's rhythmic flow
You take my hand
Nerves respond to touch
Love and desire rise
Cause my skin to blush
Special moment
Unique to our story
Gifted by life
Captured in memory

ETERNAL ROMANCE

She is old now
Years taken toll
Stiff joints
Arthritis in control
He too elderly
Ailments galore
Endless succession
Undignified bore
Standing by mirror
Laugh at reflection
Her mother, his father

Spring to recollection
Oh, but his heart sees
Girl she used to be
Faded eyes hint
At mischief, vivacity
And her spirit continues
To leap in his presence
Done so for decades
Drawn to innate benevolence
She winks, takes his hand
Invites him to dance
They shuffle to beat
Of eternal romance

TENDER CARE

You taught me to feel
What others merely see
Awakened the optimist
Dormant within me
Gave me lessons
In unconditional love
Anchored its essence

From storms above
Showed me how to open
Windows of possibilities
Slam the door shut
On doubts, uncertainties
Explained laughter, tears,
Make sense to humanity

Helped me breathe
Air of normality
Took my broken spirit
Appreciated worth
Guided it with tender care
Towards its rebirth

STOLEN KISSES

You stole a kiss
A long time ago
It was fun
Great for my ego
Met years later
Chance encounter
You decided

To steal another
Five decades on
Fate decreed
My turn
To do deed
Gave condolences

To your kin
Paid respects
At your coffin
Kissed you
For the first time
Wished Destiny
Had made you mine

DISTILLED LOVE

She hums along
To jukebox tunes
Mind revisiting
Youth's saloons
Friday their night
Cherished routine
Clings to memory

Believes herself eighteen
Lost in past
Rarely speaks
Occasionally her fingers
Brush his cheek
Wipe away a tear

On trembling tips
Presses them gently
Against her lips
Patrons watch discreetly
Catch each other's eye
In presence of distilled love
Have a tendency to cry
Toxic partnerships

TOXIC PARTNERSHIPS

My downfall
Could not resist
Your unique charm
Inherent power
To seduce, disarm
Knew it foolish
To trust you completely ignored instincts
Revealed vulnerability
Oh you were tender
For a long while
Well practiced
Hid insidious guide,
Soon took command
Of my emotions
Shattered self esteem
Caused mental confusion
Now i am expert in psychology
Understand my behavior
Your modus operandi
Yet run to your side
When you call
Distorted idea of love
My downfall

THE PROCESS

You break me
Takes a while
During the process
You smile
Chuckle internality
Search for vulnerability
Prod, dig, scoop
Expose fragility
Confuse my mind
Cruel intention
My spirit weakens
With each accusation
Leave me in a pool Of alienation
To swim, or drown in humiliation
Survive, build defenses,
You return to my orbit
Fragment me again
And I allow it

SAME DIRECTION

That was not love
Beautifully wrapped
Under layers
My spirit trapped
Suffocated by demands
Beholden to your self-image
Subservient
Under your patronage
That was not love
Although I once believed it
You pretended to care
Used me for your benefit in tiny pieces tore
Confidence away
Little bit more
Each passing day
This is love
Now i understand normal
Profound mutual respect
At deepest level
No need to measure words
Supportive affection
Two people pulling
In the same direction

SENSELESS

I may inhabit your idea
Of miserable existence
Yet am surrounded by
Light Mind free of bitterness
Finally see you clearly
Suffocating self-absorption
Aura of darkness
Lingering trail of poison

Your words conceal malice
Hidden meanings unsubtle
Manipulative strategy obvious
Narcissism remarkable
My Ego could sink
To your level
Live, breathe, spout
Unceasing vitriol
Prefers to keep afloat
Swim in calm waters
Bathing in love, empathy

All that matters
So keep provoking
Searching for vulnerability
Running around in circles
Drive yourself crazy
I am not afraid of battles
Choose carefully
This one senseless
You, and it, bore me

IN LIMBO

I never imagined
Living this way
Doubting each word
You say
Trust eroded
Increasing indifference
Spirit denuded
Of strength, resistance
Existing in increments of time
Five minutes ahead
Attempts to think beyond
Cause unbearable dread

Emotions closing down
Stagnant, in limbo
Despair kept at bay
By robotic flow
Wake, wash, eat, and sleep,
Attend to daily chores
Socialize less and less
No wish to go outdoors
Residing with a stranger
How will this end
Impossible to conceive
You were once my best friend

UPLIFTING

Everywhere
I am that swirl
Of sudden breeze
Graceful baited
Of falling leaves
I am bird song its symphony
Cries of seagulls
Circling endlessly
I am the sea
Stormy, cairn
Healing water
Refreshing brain
I am hopeful spring
Glorious summer
Resplendent autumn
Hibernating winter
I am majestic moon
Glowing stars infinite sky
Planet Mars
I am the Universe Sense
My embrace Look anywhere
See my loving face

MERRILY

Lyrical birdsong
Greets new day
Striated sky
Blue, orange, gray
Sun rises
Dazzling view
Emerald field
Bathed in dew
Gentle gusts
Sway willow tree
Trembling leaves
Rustle gently
Concealing canopy
Barefoot sprite
Dances merrily

RELEASE

These feathers
Timeworn
Eased your passage
When you were born
Held you close
Delivered your mortal body
Into destiny's embrace
I stood aside
Difficult to let go
Leave you to face
Fears, sorrow
And did my best
Precious earthly star
To protect, guide
From afar
Life's light now dims
End of this journey
I move close
Lift your unique energy
Weathered plumes
Cradle you once more
Bittersweet flight
I spread my wings
Perform final duty
Release your soul
To shine eternity

AN EMBRACE

Who are you
Little girl
Dancing, dancing
Skirt swirl
Moving to rhythm
Only you hear
Tinkling laughter
Music to my ears
I gaze at you
With envy
Eyes sense
Familiarity
You beckon
We twirl until dizzy
And, I embrace,
He child within me

ENLIGHTENMENT

Sudden deluge
Hailstone, rain
Beat against
Window pane
Gusty wind
Curtains billow
Wild dance
Dappled moon glow
She steps outside
Into nature's caress
Sighs deeply
Discards stress
Cacaphony ends
Not a sound
Silence, stillness
Surrounds
Glistening plants
Indescribable scent
Peace descends
Spiritual enlightenment

YOUTH/ OLDER ADULTS

Beautiful youth
Coffee on tap
Gallons of gin
Liven, maintain
Free spirit within
Smudged mascara
Creased clothes
Cigarette in mouth
Languid pose
Last sip of espresso
Duck shower
Adventure over
Ready for another
Raging hormones
Passion, energy
All six senses
High activity
Self-centered core
Hedonistic pleasure
Each experience
Memory to treasure
Live to fullest
Beautiful youth
Soon gone forever
Bleak, sad truth

THE BELL TOLLS

Grace and beauty
Of youth upstaged
Stealthily
By advancing age
Swollen joints creak
Muscles ache
Fragile bones
Determined to break
Oh, to dance madly
One more time
In wild abandon
Sublime!
Whirling skirt
Limber, tanned legs
In place of mottled
Unsteady pegs
To once more
Feel immortal
Believe every dream
Attainable
Enchant
Before call
To relinquish
Iife As my bell tolls

LABELS

I have arrived
At "senior years"
Term attributed
To my peers Aspirations?
Cruises galore
Downsized homes
Elegant decor
Comfortable wealth
Cleverly cut silver hair
State of art
Reclining chairs
Not me! Small pension
I'll make do
Home dyed locks
Nourishing stews
Rosy cheeks
From walks by sea
Occasional overindulgence
In G&T's
No change at all
From young adult years
Or middle aged
Hopes, dreams, fears
I remain the same
Drop labels society
I am an individual
Leave me be

LIFE’S FRAGILITY

Onto balcony
Removes shoes
Supportive, ugly
Unloosens hair

Secret vanity
Silver waves cascade
Shimmer brightly
Slowly lifts mane
Arthritic hands
Warm, gentle wind
Tousles strands
Sky darkens
Ethereal stars glow
Breathes, in rhythm,
To sea's ebb,
Flow Ageing's indignities
Forgotten temporarily
Embraces moment
Aware of life’s fragility

SURRENDER

Oh, we are beautiful,
Effervescent energy
Shimmering youth
No concept of reality
Innocent minds

Fresh faced charm
Follow idealistic pursuits
Use power to disarm
Dance, sing, dream
Of changing society
Oppose injustice

Fight for vulnerable humanity
Maturity altering priorities?
Beyond comprehension
Disappointed in parents
Dismissive of older generation

Until adulthood encroaches
Commitments, domesticity
And, we too, surrender
Baton of responsibility

YESTERDAY'S REFLECTION

Ageing relentless
Surprise to the last
Youth's essence remains
Though decades fly past
Its vigorous vitality
Resides in the mind
Deceives perception
Intention kind

Blind to wear, tear
Anatomy falling apart
Deaf to erratic beats
Of worn out hearts
Maturity's magical mirror
Allows filmy eyes to see
Yesterday's reflection
Who we are, always will be

FOUR SEASONS

Last season in cycle
Maturity
Winter approaches
Alarming velocity
Vision dims
Mind gains clarity
World, its inhabitants,
Revealed, in all absurdity
Finally comfortable
In my own skin
Opinion of others

Does not raise adrenaline
Enjoy lying fallow
Peaceful contemplation
Humanitarian battles
Left to younger generations
Life lessons learnt
Appreciate simple pleasures
To be loved, return it
The greatest treasure
Vibrancy of autumn
Possibilities in spring
Summer illusions
Tender memories within

Margaret Karim is a retired local government officer. She lives in historic Gibraltar, is passionate about words and her beloved Rock.

www.ingramcontent.com/pod-product-compliance
Lightning Source LLC
LaVergne TN
LVHW050420160826
845677LV00002BA/455

9786214708840